ARCTIC FOX

By Rachel Rose

Minneapolis, Minnesota

Credits

Cover and title page, © Alexey Seafarer/Shutterstock; 3, © DmitryND/iStock; 4, © hannurama/iStock; 4–5, © Danita Delimont/Alamy Stock Photo; 6–7, © DmitryND/iStock; 8, © All Canada Photos/Alamy Stock Photo; 8–9, © outdoorsman/Shutterstock; 11, © Kerry Hargrove/iStock; 13, © imageBROKER.com GmbH & Co. KG/Alamy Stock Photo; 14, © sanju1414/Shutterstock; 14–15, © Bjorn H Stuedal/Shutterstock; 16, © Frank Fichtmüller/Adobe Stock; 17, © Buka Pl/Adobe Stock; 18–19, © Jim Cumming/Adobe Stock; 21, © Paul/Adobe Stock; 22, © lukiv007/iStock; 23, © Menno Schaefer/Adobe Stock.

Bearport Publishing Company Product Development Team

Publisher: Jen Jenson; Director of Product Development: Spencer Brinker; Managing Editor: Allison Juda; Editor: Cole Nelson; Associate Editor: Naomi Reich; Associate Editor: Tiana Tran; Designer: Kim Jones; Designer: Kayla Eggert; Designer: Steve Scheluchin; Production Specialist: Owen Hamlin

Statement on Usage of Generative Artificial Intelligence

Bearport Publishing remains committed to publishing high-quality nonfiction books. Therefore, we restrict the use of generative AI to ensure accuracy of all text and visual components pertaining to a book's subject. See BearportPublishing.com for details.

Library of Congress Cataloging-in-Publication Data is available at www.loc.gov or upon request from the publisher.

ISBN: 979-8-89577-043-6 (hardcover)
ISBN: 979-8-89577-467-0 (paperback)
ISBN: 979-8-89577-160-0 (ebook)

Copyright © 2026 Bearport Publishing Company. All rights reserved. No part of this publication may be reproduced in whole or in part, stored in any retrieval system, or transmitted in any form or by any means, electronic, mechanical, photocopying, recording, or otherwise, without written permission from the publisher. Bearport Publishing is a division of FlutterBee Education Group.

For more information, write to Bearport Publishing, 5357 Penn Avenue South, Minneapolis, MN 55419.

Contents

Awesome Arctic Foxes! 4
Baby, It's Cold Outside 6
A Warm Blanket 8
Home Sweet Home 10
Spring Colors 12
Small Fox, Big Danger 14
On the Hunt 16
Catch Me If You Can 18
Cute Kits 20

Information Station 22
Glossary 23
Index 24
Read More 24
Learn More Online 24
About the Author 24

AWESOME
Arctic Foxes!

An arctic fox leaps into the air and dives headfirst into the snow. **CRUNCH!** The fox closes its mouth around the small mouse it heard scurrying under the snow. Quick and **agile**, arctic foxes are awesome!

THE ACT OF POUNCING ON **PREY** FROM ABOVE IS CALLED MOUSING.

Baby, It's Cold Outside

As their name suggests, these foxes live in the Arctic—one of the harshest places on the planet. With record lows dipping down to –94 degrees Fahrenheit (–70°C), the Arctic is frigid. *BRRR!* But an arctic fox's small size helps the cute creature stay warm. That's because tiny bodies lose less heat to the cold.

ARCTIC FOXES CAN WEIGH UP TO 17 POUNDS (7 KG). THAT'S LIGHTER THAN A LARGE WATERMELON!

A Warm Blanket

Being small isn't the only way arctic foxes stay warm in their chilly **habitat**. The animals are also covered in thick fur all over their bodies. At night, the foxes wrap their long, fluffy tails around themselves. The tails act as a blanket to keep them extra toasty and safe from the cold.

FUR ON THE BOTTOM OF AN ARCTIC FOX'S PAWS PROTECTS ITS FEET—JUST LIKE LITTLE SNOW BOOTS!

Home Sweet Home

Arctic foxes live in underground homes called dens. They usually build their dens under mounds of snow, beneath rock piles, or at the base of hills. Arctic fox dens can have a few entrances with lots of tunnels and rooms. The tunnels in these underground homes can be as long as several football fields put together!

ARCTIC FOXES STAY SAFE IN THEIR DENS WHEN WINTER STORMS MAKE IT TOO DIFFICULT TO HUNT.

A den entrance

Spring Colors

When spring comes and the snow starts to melt, the arctic fox's fur begins to change. Its long, thick coat sheds to a short, thin one. And instead of white, the fox's spring and summer fur is gray, brown, or bluish-brown. These darker colors help the animal **camouflage** with the grasses and plants that replace the snow.

DARK COLORS HELP ARCTIC FOXES BLEND IN WITH ROCKS, TOO.

Small Fox, Big Danger

Blending in with their surroundings helps arctic foxes hide from **predators**. Many animals hunt the furry foxes, including golden eagles, arctic wolves, polar bears, and grizzly bears. However, animals are not the only **threat**. The Arctic is warming almost three times faster than the rest of the world, and the rapidly melting snow means a loss of the arctic fox's habitat.

A golden eagle

On the Hunt

Lemmings, a favorite food of arctic foxes, live under the snow. As the Arctic warms and more snow melts, the little animals may go elsewhere. This leaves arctic foxes with a limited food supply. To survive, the foxes will often eat whatever they can find, including berries, birds, and insects. **YUM!**

A lemming

Catch Me If You Can

When it's time to **mate**, arctic foxes will play-fight and chase each other around. They yowl to communicate over long distances with their partners. About seven weeks after mating, the **female** will give birth. She usually has about 8 babies, but a fox mom can sometimes have as many as 25 at once! This is one of the largest **litter** sizes of any animal in the wild.

ARCTIC FOXES USUALLY KEEP THE SAME PARTNER FOR LIFE.

Cute Kits

Arctic fox parents work together to raise their babies, called kits. The **male** will guard the den as the newborn kits drink their mother's milk. When they are around three months old, the young foxes are ready to go out and hunt for themselves. After 10 months, they are fully grown and ready to start families of their own.

ARCTIC FOXES LIVE FOR ONLY ABOUT THREE TO SIX YEARS.

Information Station

ARCTIC FOXES ARE AWESOME!
LET'S LEARN MORE ABOUT THEM.

Kind of animal: Arctic foxes are mammals. Most mammals have fur, give birth to live young, and drink milk from their mothers as babies.

Other foxes: Arctic foxes are one of several **species** of true foxes found around the world. This group also includes red foxes, silver foxes, and fennec foxes.

Size: Arctic foxes grow up to 12 inches (30 cm) in height. That's about as tall as a cereal box!

ARCTIC FOXES AROUND THE WORLD

▢ Where Arctic Foxes Live

Glossary

agile able to move quickly and easily

camouflage to blend in or hide by looking the same as one's surroundings

female an arctic fox that can give birth to young

habitat a place in nature where an animal is usually found

litter a group of animals born at the same time to the same mother

male an arctic fox that cannot give birth to young

mate to come together in order to have young

predators animals that hunt and kill other animals for food

prey an animal that is hunted and eaten by other animals

species groups that animals are divided into according to similar characteristics

threat someone or something that might cause harm

Index

Arctic 6, 14, 16
dens 10, 20
female 18
habitat 8, 14
kits 20
male 20

mate 18–19
predators 14
prey 4, 16
snow 4, 8, 10, 12, 14, 16
species 22
threat 14–15

Read More

Miller, Marie-Therese. *Sly as a Fox: Are Foxes Clever? (Animal Idioms).* North Mankato, MN: Abdo Publishing, 2022.

Starr, Abbe L. *Arctic Ice Loss (Spotlight on Climate Change).* Minneapolis: Lerner Publications, 2023.

Learn More Online

1. Go to **FactSurfer.com** or scan the QR code below.
2. Enter "**Arctic Fox**" into the search box.
3. Click on the cover of this book to see a list of websites.

About the Author

Rachel Rose writes books for kids and teaches yoga. Her favorite animal of all is her dog, Sandy.